The Great Watermelon Contest

Brenda Parkes
Illustrated by Kevin Serwacki

Rigby
A Harcourt Achieve Imprint

www.Rigby.com
1-800-531-5015

Anna, Sara, and Paul were neighbors. They were also all prize-winning gardeners. Anna grew the juiciest apples. Sara grew the sweetest strawberries. And Paul grew the biggest pumpkins around.

One year, all three neighbors entered the town watermelon contest. Only one person could win first prize, so each neighbor began a secret plan to grow the winning watermelon.

Anna thought of ways to make her watermelon look fun and special.

Sara wanted to grow a giant watermelon.

Paul planned to grow a
watermelon in a strange shape.

They kept their plans secret.

Anna built
a special
shed to hide
her prize
watermelon.

Sara built
a tall fence
to hide
her prize
watermelon.

Paul hired an elephant to keep people from spying on his prize watermelon!

The three neighbors watched each other every day.

What was Anna
doing with
pieces of cloth
and glue?

What was
Sara doing
with a
measuring
tape?

What was Paul doing with such large boxes?

The three neighbors were so busy watching each other, they didn't think about anyone else in the contest.

Bobby Jenkins was a new gardener in town. His grandpa was teaching him how to grow great watermelons.

"Just remember that all a watermelon really needs is water, sun, and love," said Bobby's grandpa.

At last it was time for the contest. There were more sizes and shapes of watermelons than you could imagine!

Anna showed her watermelon first. The crowd clapped. Anna's watermelon had a smiling face!

Sara showed her watermelon next. The crowd cheered. Her watermelon was huge!

Then Paul showed his
watermelon. The crowd gasped.
His watermelon was in the
shape of a cube!

Bobby showed his watermelon last. It was a regular watermelon, but it was perfect.

The judge of the contest wrinkled her brow. Each watermelon was so wonderful in its own way. How could she choose a winner?

"Isn't taste the most important thing?" shouted a boy in the crowd.

"Good idea," said the judge. "Children can taste each watermelon to decide who the winner will be!"

First they tasted Anna's
watermelon. The judge cut
several slices. The children
each took a bite. Juice dripped
from their fingers.

"Mmmm," they said.

Anna took a bow.

Next they tasted Sara's watermelon. The judge climbed a stepstool and cut a slice. The children bit into big chunks. Juice dripped from their chins.

"Mmmm," they said.

Sara smiled proudly.

Paul's watermelon was next.
Eagerly the children took bites.
Juice dripped from their wrists.
"Mmmm," they said.
Paul waved to the crowd.

Bobby Jenkins smiled as he waited for the judge to slice his watermelon. The judge looked at the small, round watermelon for a moment.

As the judge cut a slice, the warm, sweet smell of a summer breeze filled the air. The children took bites. Juice ran down to their elbows.

"Mmmm! Mmmm! Mmmm!" they
shouted. "This one is the best
of all!"

The judge stuck a blue
ribbon on Bobby's shirt. "What's
your secret?" she asked.

"Water, sun, and love, like Grandpa told me," said Bobby.